Movements in Art **THE BAROQUE PERIOD**

Movements in Art THE BAROQUE PERIOD

ANNE FITZPATRICK

CREATIVE EDUCATION

Published by Creative Education
123 South Broad Street, Mankato, Minnesota 56001
Creative Education is an imprint of The Creative Company

Design and production by Blue Design (www.bluedes.com)
Art direction by Rita Marshall

Photographs by Art Resource, NY (Nimatallah) Corbis (Alinari Archives,
Paul Almasy, James L. Amos, Archivo Iconografico, S.A., Arte & Immagini
srl, Bettmann, Alexander Burkatovski, Burstein Collection, Peter Harholdt,
John Heseltine, Historical Picture Archive, Hulton-Deutsch Collection, David
Lees, Massimo Listri, Araldo de Luca, Francis G. Mayer, National Gallery
Collection; By kind permission of the Trustees of the National Gallery,
London, Gianni Dagli Orti, Hans Georg Roth, World Films Enterprises)

Library of Congress Cataloging-in-Publication Data

Fitzpatrick, Anne, 1978–
The Baroque period / by Anne Fitzpatrick.
p. cm. — (Movements in art)
Includes index.
ISBN 1-58341-346-4
1. Art, Baroque—Juvenile literature. I. Title. II. Series.

N6415.B3F57 2005
709'.032—dc22   2004056241

First edition

9 8 7 6 5 4 3 2 1

Cover: **The Consequences of War** *by Peter Paul Rubens (1638)*
Page 2: **Belshazzar's Feast** *by Rembrandt van Rijn (1635)*
Pages 4–5: **Minerva Protects Pax from Mars** *by Rubens (1629–30)*

Baroque art developed against a background of turmoil within the religious world. It was at this time that the Catholic Church convened the Council of Trent to reexamine and declare its doctrine.

The Baroque Period

The history of the world can be told through accounts of great battles, the lives of kings and queens, and the discoveries and inventions of scientists and explorers. But the history of the way people think and feel about themselves and the world is told through art. From paintings of the hunt in prehistoric caves, to sacred art in the European Middle Ages, to the abstract forms of the 20th century, movements in art are the expression of a culture. Sometimes that expression is so powerful and compelling that it reaches through time to carry its message to another generation.

The powerful line of Bourbon kings, who ruled France from 1589 to 1792 and 1815 to 1830, presided during the Baroque period, leading France to become a world power and a leader in the arts.

From opportunities to sail to America in search of a new and prosperous future, to new scientific discoveries, Europeans of the 16th and 17th centuries faced intense changes to their worldview.

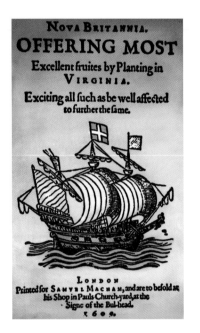

Baroque art is the message of a people who were trying to make sense of a world that was changing faster every day. It is the style of an international **diplomat**, traveling Europe to bring peace to warring nations and expressing his idealism in the intense symbolism of his paintings. It is the style of a moody renegade, fleeing from the law and turning his anguish into passionate, spiritual masterpieces. It is the style of close confidantes of kings and popes, working in the shadow of immense power. The grandeur and intensity of Baroque art is a reaction to dramatic transformations in 17th-century European science, religion, politics, and society. As the march of history continues, it is a message that resonates with every new generation.

A NEW WORLD

When Christopher Columbus landed on an island in the Caribbean in 1492, he announced that he had found a "New World." As Europeans began to **colonize** North and South America, Columbus's phrase was often used to describe the continents they'd never known existed. But Europe itself became a "New World" in the centuries that followed Columbus's discovery. Politics, religion, society, and culture underwent profound changes that marked the beginning of modern history.

GALILEO GALILEI

Galileo Galilei was born to a noble family in Pisa, Italy, in 1564. He became fascinated by mathematics and physics while a college student and made many important discoveries. Galileo was also a gifted inventor. One of his inventions was a telescope, which he used to look at the stars and planets. His observations confirmed Copernicus's theory that Earth revolved around the sun. In 1633, after he published a book announcing his findings, the Catholic Church summoned him to Rome. They charged him with heresy, or holding a belief specifically denounced by the Church. He was sentenced to house arrest for the remainder of his life and died at his home in Florence in 1642.

With the posting of his Ninety-five Theses, Martin Luther (left) started a series of religious discussions among both the clergy and the common people, which ultimately resulted in the splintering of the Church and the formation of Protestant denominations.

In 1632, the Italian astronomer Galileo Galilei published a book in which he argued that the sun was the center of the universe. The theory had already been suggested in 1543 by Polish astronomer Nicolaus Copernicus, but it met with resistance and even ridicule. The accepted account was that the sun revolved around the Earth. If Copernicus and Galileo were right, the universe was much larger—perhaps infinitely so—than previously thought. It also presented crucial problems for contemporary Christianity: if Earth revolved around the sun, where were God and Heaven? And how could humanity be the culmination of creation, given dominion over all else, if it was not even at the center of the universe? Although religious leaders denounced the theory, Europeans' ideas about their place in the universe had begun to change.

Christianity was already in turmoil because of a movement known as the Protestant Reformation. Growing dissatisfaction with the Catholic Church led to the splintering of Christianity beginning in 1517. That year, a German friar named Martin Luther attacked the Church's practice of selling people "indulgences"—forgiveness without penalties—for their sins. He argued that only personal faith could justify forgiveness of sins. He rejected the Church's claim to speak for God and declared that the Bible was the only true authority. Luther's "protest" of Catholicism led to the creation of several new Christian religions, collectively known as Protestant faiths. Europe was torn by decades of war as Catholics and Protestants fought for political control. When the dust settled, the winner was unclear. French, Spanish, and Italian Catholics controlled some parts of Europe, and German, Dutch, and Swiss Protestants controlled others.

THE AGE OF COLONIALISM

European exploration of the Americas quickly turned to colonization and conquest. As explorers "discovered" new lands, they claimed them as territories of their homelands. Soon, boatloads of people arrived to build settlements and sow crops. By 1600, the Spanish laid claim to more land than any one kingdom had ever before claimed. The settlers established themselves as rulers and landlords over the Native American

people. Many Native Americans died from the new diseases brought by Europeans, and the need for labor on the vast farms being established in the Americas fueled the African slave trade. European empire-building was becoming the dominant force in a world that suddenly seemed much smaller.

PLACE TO VISIT: CHÂTEAU DE VERSAILLES

A short train ride from Paris, the Palace of Versailles was once home to 20,000 nobles and their servants—as well as King Louis XIV. Today, the palace is a museum open to the public. One can tour the formal rooms of state, such as the elaborately decorated Hall of Mirrors, as well as the

more intimate apartments in which the royal family lived. The Royal **Chapel**, where the king attended mass, is particularly striking, with its delicately carved, white stone pillars and arches decorated with masses of brilliant **gilt**. The gardens cover 250 acres (100 ha) with elegant flowerbeds, fountains, lakes, lawns, and woods. Marie-Antoniette's Arcadian village can also be seen.

Religion continued to play a central role in Europeans' lives, although it was no longer dominated by the Catholic Church. But the Church did not surrender easily. In some ways, its influence was more apparent during the 17th century than in the years leading up to the Reformation, as Church officials fought to regain their former prominence. At the Council of Trent, a meeting of Church officials in northern Italy that began in 1545 and continued until 1563, Catholic teachings and authority were redefined and reasserted. The importance of inspiring and instructing the faithful was emphasized. In particular, the Church wanted to appeal to the large and powerful middle class that was emerging. The new class had come into being as life became more centered on towns and trade and the agricultural system of rich landlords and poor tenants declined.

These changes in society also contributed to the formation of powerful nation-states. During the 17th century, the feudal system, in which many lesser rulers controlled their own lands and paid tribute to a king or emperor, was replaced by systems of government based on a single, centralized authority. King Louis XIV of France built a palace at Versailles and required French **nobles** to live there for at least part of the year, making it the center of government for all of France. King Philip II of Spain built a huge monastery and palace near Madrid, where he tried personally to keep track of an empire that stretched all the way to South America. The monarchs increased their power by introducing national taxes to pay for large armies. The idea of sovereignty–that there was only one ultimate law-making authority in any given area, and it was all-powerful–began to take hold.

CONCILIO TRIDENTINO
PERFECTO
SANCTA SYNODUS OMNIUM QVÆ IN
EO DECRETA ERANT CONFIRMATIONEM
A ROM. PONT. MAX. PER
APOSTOLICÆ SEDIS LEGATOS
PETIT

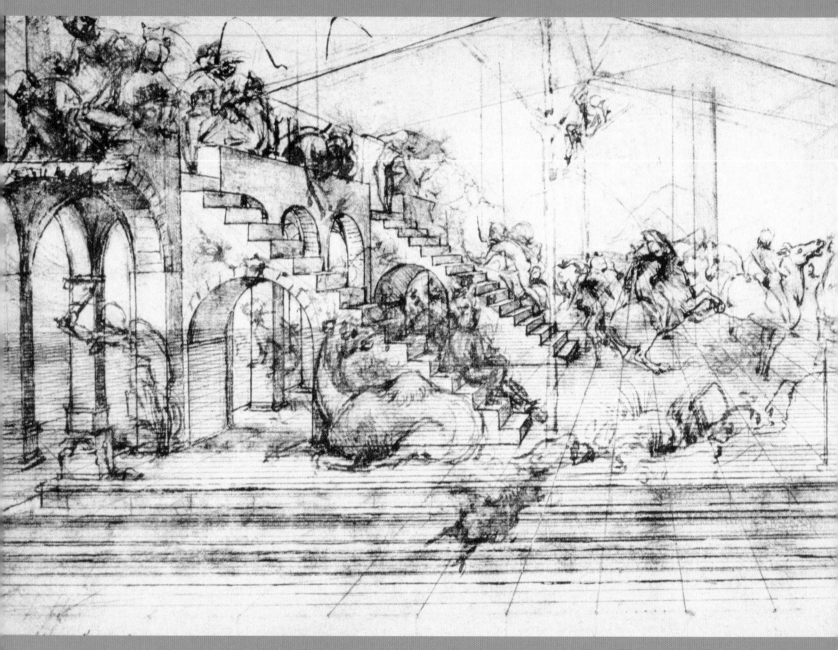

Renaissance artist Leonardo da Vinci was a pioneer in the development of perspective. In this preliminary study, he was experimenting with the perspective of animals and figures he planned to use in a later piece.

These changes in European society were accompanied by great changes in art. During the 15th century and the first half of the 16th, an artistic movement known as the Renaissance broke away from medieval styles and announced the beginning of "modern" style. Artists turned to the art of **Classical** Rome and Greece, embracing its formal rules and emphasis on balance and harmony. They focused on creating more faithful depictions of nature and developed new techniques of **perspective** and shading to portray space and volume. Leonardo da Vinci, Michelangelo Buonarroti, Raphael Sanzio, and others created some of the world's greatest masterpieces. But as the 16th century progressed, artists showed increasing freedom in depicting their own interpretations, feelings, and ideas, instead of trying to depict reality or create harmony. They played with the restrictive rules of formal, Classical art, intentionally breaking them and deliberately distorting figures in order to produce heightened artistic or emotional effects. This **decadent** style, called Mannerism, was short-lived. By the end of the 16th century, artists were ready for something new.

In 1589, in Bologna, Italy, Annibale Caracci (1560–1609), with his brother and uncle, founded a school of art called the Accademia degli Incamminati, or "Academy of the Right Road." They wanted to reform art by returning to the example of past masters such as Michelangelo, Raphael, and Titian, and by studying **anatomy** and drawing from live models. Their reform was extremely successful, and the academy attracted many students. In 1598, Cardinal Odoardo Farnese, a high-ranking official in the Catholic Church, asked Caracci to decorate the Farnese family palace in Rome.

The ceiling **fresco** Caracci painted in a gallery of the palace was the first great masterpiece of a new style: the Baroque. The fresco depicted

Raphael's focus on human anatomy can be seen in this drawing of a child, a sketch created for a later work. The careful attention to the intricacies of the human form, including muscles and flesh, was characteristic of Renaissance art.

In creating his fresco on the Farnese palace ceiling, Caracci influenced Baroque artists both with his representation of the heroic figure and with his artistic technique, which involved the creation of hundreds of preparatory drawings.

Although he was one of the first painters of the Baroque style, Annibale Caracci's artistic career was short, as he suffered from extreme depression and gave up painting almost entirely in 1606, only two years after finishing this self-portrait. When he died, he was buried near the Renaissance master Raphael, according to his wishes.

joyful, sensuous scenes from the *Metamorphoses*, a collection of myths by the ancient Roman poet Ovid. Caracci took Renaissance techniques to new heights, using light, shadow, and perspective to create the illusion of three-dimensional carving, statues, and open sky on the flat ceiling. He revived the Classical idea that art is about the relationships and interactions of shapes, but brought new life to the careful arrangements with a crackling sense of energy and movement. The fresco was immediately celebrated as the equal of great Renaissance masterpieces.

In *The Mystic Marriage of St. Catherine* (1585–87), which was once part of the Farnese collection, Caracci used a dark background to better emphasize the soft light that streams in from one side of the painting.

In another part of Rome, Michelangelo Merisi, known as Caravaggio (1573–1610) after his birthplace in northern Italy, brought new life to painting with a very different approach. He was hard at work between 1597 and 1601 on three paintings depicting the life of St. Matthew for the Contarelli Chapel in the Church of San Luigi dei Francesi. The stark **realism** he employed to portray the holy scenes shocked and even offended many people. Backgrounds and settings were virtually eliminated, leaving only the solid, physical presence of the human figures. The play of light and shadow in the

The muted tones and grave nature of Caracci's *Lamentation of Christ* (1603–04) show the influence of not only Renaissance artists such as Michelangelo and Raphael, but also of the Classical works that surrounded the artist in Rome.

Caravaggio's *The Calling of St. Matthew* captures the moment when Jesus and Peter enter the room where Matthew is sitting with the other tax collectors. Jesus gestures to call Matthew, who seems incredulous that he has been chosen.

PLACE TO VISIT: CHURCHES OF ROME

Rome's innumerable churches are treasure troves of Baroque art. San Luigi dei Francesi is dominated by Caravaggio's inspired paintings of the life of St. Matthew. Nearby, Chiesa del Gesù was built to answer the post-Reformation need for large, impressive churches. It boasts an amazing ceiling fresco that displays the Baroque passion for illusion in its depictions of sculptures, decorative carving, and open sky. Santa Maria

della Vittoria, in addition to housing Bernini's Coronaro Chapel and *Ecstasy of St. Theresa*, is richly decorated with colorful marble and gilt in classic Baroque style. Another chapel designed by Bernini is located in Santa Maria del Popolo, alongside two of Caravaggio's best-known paintings: *The Crucifixion of St. Peter* (1601) and *The Conversion of St. Paul* (1600). (Pictured: *Ecstasy of St. Theresa*)

paintings is extreme, plunging the background into darkness out of which the figures emerge in dramatic spotlights. In the *Calling of St. Matthew* (1598–99), Jesus is relegated to the background, with no halo or other sign of his identity. The only indication of a divine presence is a cross created by a window frame and lit by a diagonal shaft of light. Caravaggio's intense realism was the counterpoint to Caracci's Classical revival. These became the two central themes of the Baroque movement, creating a fruitful exchange that gave rise to a large variety of styles.

ARTISTS OF THE BAROQUE PERIOD

Caravaggio began his artistic career at age 11, when he became an orphan and was **apprenticed** to a painter in Milan. Sometime between the ages of 15 and 19, he made his way to Rome. Penniless and alone, he nevertheless managed to continue painting. After about five years, he came to the attention of Cardinal Francesco Del Monte, an influential member of the pope's court. Cardinal Del Monte became his **patron** and got him the **commission** for the decoration of the Contarelli Chapel. The completed project made him both famous and infamous, offending as many people as it captivated.

Peter Paul Rubens painted *The Consequences of War* (1637–38) at a time when he feared that his homeland was on the brink of battle. The work depicts a woman shielding her child from the wrath of Mars, the god of war.

PLACE TO VISIT: RUBENS HOUSE

After Rubens moved to Antwerp in 1608, he bought a house and turned it into a showpiece of Italian Baroque architecture. Today, the house is a museum, restored to appear as it did when Rubens lived there. The impressive entrance is through an ornate gate into a courtyard overlooked by a highly decorated façade. An open gallery connects the living quarters to the artist's workshop, where large,

round windows overlook an elegant garden. Inside the house, a collection of paintings by Rubens and some of his contemporaries is on display. Antwerp also offers more than 20 Rubens paintings at the Royal Museum of Fine Arts, and three of Rubens's **altarpieces** in Our Lady's Cathedral, including the *Descent from the Cross*.

Caravaggio remained a controversial painter throughout his career. His masterpiece, *Death of the Virgin* (1605–06), was refused by the church that had commissioned it because the peasant-like features, bare legs, and obvious pregnancy of the Virgin Mary shocked the priests. Caravaggio's personal life was controversial as well. Gloomy and violent, he was frequently in trouble with the law. In 1606, he killed a man in a fight and had to flee Rome. He moved around southern Italy and the Mediterranean islands, continuing to work on paintings that were increasingly dark and intense. Caravaggio died in 1610, three days before a letter pardoning his crime arrived from the pope.

A painter named Peter Paul Rubens (1577–1640), who was working for the Duke of Mantua, persuaded the duke to purchase Caravaggio's *Death of the Virgin* after it was rejected by the priests. The collection of art at Mantua was the second-best in Europe—only the pope's was better—and Rubens had many opportunities to study the works of great painters there. Throughout his life, his work as a diplomat took him all over Europe and gave him access to the masterpieces of Rome, Madrid, and Paris, among others.

Rubens was originally from Antwerp, in present-day Belgium, but his family lived in Germany for most of his childhood to escape persecution for the Protestant sympathies of his father, a diplomat and scholar. When Rubens was 10 years old, his father died. The family returned to Antwerp, where Rubens worked briefly at the court of a countess before being apprenticed as a painter. He left Antwerp at the age of 23, intent on studying the art of the Italian Renaissance. After eight years in the service of the Duke of Mantua, he returned to Antwerp to become a court painter and diplomat for the Spanish rulers of Flanders (present-day Belgium and the Netherlands). Despite his

Although Velázquez's original portrait of King Philip IV has been lost, this portrait (detail, opposite) from around 1628 is one of the first he painted after becoming the king's official portraitist. While the portrait is grand and dignified, it also shows the artist's ability to bring life and character to his figures.

extensive travels, Rubens was a prolific painter, known for his inventiveness and energy. On one of his diplomatic missions, Rubens painted *Peace and War* (1629–30) to convince King Charles I of England to choose peace. It was an effective strategy—soon afterward, the king signed a treaty with Spain.

Rubens was probably responsible for inspiring the Spanish painter Diego Velázquez (1599–1660) to travel to Italy. Velázquez left to study art in Genoa, Milan, Venice, Florence, and Rome shortly after Rubens spent six months at the court in Madrid on a diplomatic mission. Velázquez was the official painter to Philip IV, a post he won in 1623 after executing a portrait of the king. Philip was so taken with it that he declared that only Velázquez should paint his portrait. The painter developed a close relationship with Philip, becoming a trusted advisor.

Born in Seville to minor nobles, Velázquez was apprenticed at an early age to the Mannerist painter Francisco Pancheco. Pancheco became his father-in-law and later his biographer, but Velázquez quickly abandoned the Mannerist style. His paintings display a faithful realism and dramatic use of light similar to Caravaggio's, but his **compositions** are balanced and elegant. Velázquez employed the same perfect artistry in carefully depicting the sumptuous materials of his subjects' clothing as in capturing the playful glint or somber melancholy of their expressions.

Rembrandt van Rijn (1606–69) was known for his penetrating, sympathetic portrayals of human emotion and weakness. He recorded his own life in approximately 80 introspective **self-portraits**. Rembrandt was born in Leiden, near Amsterdam. The son of a wealthy miller, he began studying at a university, destined to be a clergyman. He showed such talent at drawing,

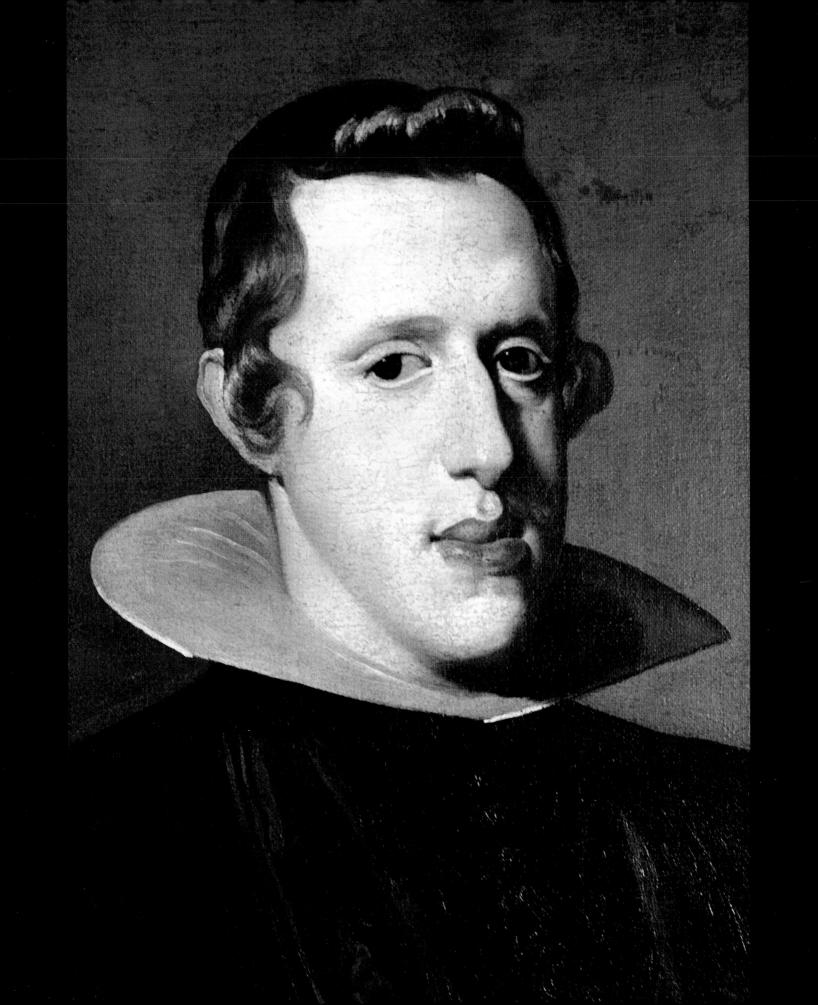

In his self-portraits, Rembrandt used a limited palette of colors, instead evoking the feeling of the painting through a variety of poses and facial expressions. This self-portrait is from 1661, when the artist was 55 years old.

however, that his father allowed him to attend a school of painting instead.

After establishing his reputation in Leiden, Rembrandt moved to Amsterdam. The city was the bustling capital of the **republic** of the Netherlands, newly free from Spanish rule. A flourishing sea trade created a wealthy class of merchants eager to adorn their houses. Rembrandt's paintings were sought after, and he soon grew rich. In his *Self-portrait with Saskia* (c. 1636), the painter is gaily costumed in fancy clothes, posed at a table in a manner that suggests he is embracing his wife. But as Rembrandt's work became more psychological and less realistic, his popularity declined. In 1657, he was forced to sell his house and furniture to pay off his debts. In one of his last self-portraits, the painter's expression is philosophical, his eyes in shadow.

The French painter Nicolas Poussin (1594–1665) was often misunderstood and underestimated by his contemporaries. His first major commission, an altarpiece for the pope in Rome, was received with such disfavor that a second commission was withdrawn. Poussin apparently accepted that such monumental work was not his strength, and spent the rest of his life working on smaller paintings. Their size was more suitable for his subdued, intellectual work, composed with deep thought and strict precision. Poussin studied literary texts, painstakingly created elaborate models, and made numerous sketches before beginning a painting. The style of each piece was carefully

In his early etching *Self-Portrait with Saskia* (1636), Rembrandt depicted himself with his new wife, Saskia, who became one of his favorite models. Rembrandt's love for his wife can be seen in the many images he created of her before her death in 1642, only eight years after they had married.

URBAN RENEWAL

The emergence of cities and the centralization of power within them sparked a new interest in city planning during the Baroque period. Officials created wide, straight avenues that met in well-defined, open spaces. In Rome, the new avenues were used to connect the city's seven major churches. They also brought new life to areas outside the city center. The city was beautified by new statues and fountains in elegant piazzas. In France, fashionable squares were created by the construction of uniform buildings around a central open space, often embellished with a statue in the center. The city walls of Paris were torn down and replaced by circular avenues that formed a series of rings radiating out from the city center.

adapted to its subject. His paintings often explored profound philosophical, religious, and moral issues with the depth and intricacy of a scholarly treatise. At the same time, they are beautiful, even sensuous, works of art.

The son of farmers, Poussin first became interested in art when an artist arrived in his small hometown on the Seine to produce several paintings for the local church. The 18-year-old was inspired to become a painter, and set off for Paris to find a teacher. After studying in Paris and Rouen, he went to Rome in 1624, drawn by reproductions he had seen of Raphael's work. The paintings of Raphael, Titian, and other Renaissance masters, as well as the collections of ancient Roman art that he saw in Rome, had a profound influence on his work. Poussin remained in Rome for the rest of his life, returning to Paris only once for a brief visit.

Gianlorenzo Bernini (1598–1680) began his career in Rome, in the sculpture workshop of his father. He established his reputation as the most important sculptor in Italy by the age of 26 with a series of statues depicting Classical myths. One of these, *Apollo and Daphne* (1622–24), is carved with such subtlety that the flesh of the maiden Daphne can be seen turning to bark as she is transformed into a tree. Bernini was also an accomplished architect, and many of his works combine the two art forms. By controlling the architectural setting of his sculptures, he could use the effects of light and shadow as part of a piece. The fountains he designed for some of Rome's great piazzas, or public squares, similarly use the movement and reflective surfaces of water to enhance the fountains' sculptured figures.

In 1629, Bernini became the official architect for St. Peter's Basilica, the pope's cathedral in Rome. He was responsible for supervising the decoration

of the interior of the church and designing its grand piazza. He personally sculpted the marble, bronze, and gilt baldacchino, a ceremonial structure that rises four stories above the altar. Bernini drew on his Roman Catholic faith to inspire his work throughout his life. He strongly believed that art should be used to touch the emotions of viewers with religious awe and guide them to worship and prayer. Bernini was an important part of the artistic push to revive the Catholic Church. Over the course of his lifetime, he served eight popes.

Gianlorenzo Bernini's *Fountain of the Four Rivers* (1648–51) in Rome is made of four marble figures symbolizing four major rivers of the world, including the Ganges (above). Although it is not known how much of the fountain Bernini actually sculpted, it is clear that the design was his and that he supervised construction.

Both painting and sculpture flourished during the Baroque period under the influence of masters such as Caravaggio, who painted the religious *Supper at Emmaus* (opposite), and Bernini, who sculpted the pagan *Apollo and Daphne* (below).

GREAT WORKS OF THE BAROQUE PERIOD

At the Council of Trent, the pope announced that art should be used to stimulate faith in the Church. The announcement created a demand for religious paintings that could draw the viewer in by appealing to the senses, yet deliver a spiritual message. Caravaggio was very successful at this, but his paintings were sometimes thought too savage or intense. Many, such as *Supper at Emmaus* (1601), were

considered irreverent because the saints and holy figures were depicted as ordinary peasants. But Caravaggio intended the youthful, beardless face of Jesus to be almost unrecognizable, so that viewers became participants in the emotional impact of the scene. After Jesus was crucified, two of his disciples met him on the road. Not knowing who he was, they invited him to eat with them. The painting shows the moment when Jesus blesses the bread, and the disciples recognize him with shock and amazement. Foreshortening—a technique that makes painted forms look as if they are coming straight out of a picture—is used on the disciple's outstretched arm. The painting's realism helps to bridge the invisible barrier between the world of the painting and that of the viewer. At the same time, Caravaggio distorted the portrayal of the light, compromising the picture's realism, in order to create a shadow halo around Jesus's head.

Rubens preferred large-scale projects such as the *Descent from the Cross*, the center panel alone (pictured) of which is larger than 13 feet by 10 feet (4 x 3 m). The piece was created for the Antwerp Cathedral in his hometown and established Rubens's reputation as the greatest painter in Flanders.

Toward the end of the 16th century, the religious art in many Catholic churches in northern Europe had been badly damaged by Protestants, and church officials were eager to create new symbols of Catholic faith. Rubens painted several altarpieces for churches in the region, including his stirring masterpiece, the *Descent from the Cross* (1612–14). In the central picture of the piece, St. John, the Virgin Mary, Mary Magdalene, and several others take Jesus off the cross after his crucifixion. Their distraught gazes and outstretched arms point the viewer's eye toward his suffering expression. A group of soldiers commissioned the painting as part of an altarpiece for the Antwerp Cathedral to honor their patron saint, Christopher. The three panels of the altarpiece—the Virgin Mary pregnant with Christ, Simeon holding the infant Jesus at his baptism, and Christ's body lifted from the cross—play on the name Christopher, which means "Christ-bearer." When the two hinged side panels of the altarpiece are closed, a painting of St. Christopher carrying the child Jesus that decorates the backs of the panels can be seen.

In parts of Europe where Protestants prevailed, religious art fell into disfavor because it was associated with idol worship and the corruption of the Catholic Church. Scenes from the Bible, however, continued to be popular because of the Protestant emphasis on scripture. Rembrandt was well-known for his deeply felt, dramatic portrayals of Biblical stories. In *Belshazzar's Feast* (c. 1635), the Babylonian king is terrified at the sight of a ghostly hand writing on the wall. The writing is God's warning to Belshazzar, who has served wine to his guests in gold and silver cups stolen from the Jewish temple. The figures are large and close to the viewer, and the woman backing away from Belshazzar's startled movement is foreshortened, seeming to project

One of Bernini's most popular sculptures, the life-sized *Apollo and Daphne* depicts the exact moment in the Greek myth when Apollo catches up with Daphne, who, wishing to escape his love, is transformed into a tree. She sprouts delicate leaves from her fingers and hair and is encircled by bark.

from the painting. With the theatrical lighting and the dramatic gestures and expressions, the effect is electrifying.

Poussin's *The Arcadian Shepherds* (c. 1638) appeals to the viewer's intellect rather than his or her emotions. The lighting is subdued, creating a contemplative mood. Arcadia was a land in ancient Greece that came to represent an earthly version of paradise, where people lived peacefully and happily in a state of rural simplicity. In the painting, four shepherds gather around a tomb, which is inscribed "Et in Arcadia Ego," meaning "I am also in Arcadia." The painting captures the inevitability of death—even in an earthly paradise. The point is emphasized by the shepherd's shadow, falling upon the inscription. The painting is composed with precision and balance; the gestures and gazes of the shepherds focus attention on the tomb, and the arrangement of their poses is echoed by the trees and mountains.

Ecstasy of St. Theresa (1646–52), Bernini's sculpture group for the Coronaro Chapel in Rome, is arranged in a dramatic composition worthy of a painting. Two groups of statues, portraits of the Coronaro family who commissioned the work, sit in balcony-like recesses on either side of the chapel. Green and red marble on the walls creates a colorful background. At the altar, St. Theresa closes her eyes in ecstasy as an angel prepares to pierce her heart with an arrow of divine love. The two figures are skillfully arranged so that they appear to float in the air. Natural light enters the chapel from an unseen opening above them, highlighting the saint's upturned face and glinting off gilt rods that represent a heavenly glow. Viewers stepping into the chapel join the figures in the balconies as they share this mystical, transcendent moment.

Velázquez created a participatory experience for a very specific audience in *Las Meninas* (1656). The focus of the painting is the five-year-old daughter of King Philip IV of Spain, Margarita, flanked by her maids of honor ("Las Meninas"). The left side of the painting is blocked by the back of a canvas. Velázquez himself, partially obscured by shadows, stands before it with his paintbrush. A mirror on the back wall shows the subject of the painting on which he works: the king and queen. They stand where the viewer stands—and where the king and queen, for whom it was painted, would have stood to view it. Margarita and her attendants gaze at the royal couple as they pose for their portrait. With this playful riddle of a painting, Velázquez portrays himself as part of an intimate family scene; it is a reminder to the king that he is a trusted, but respectful, member of the royal household.

Art and architecture were important to the royal courts of the 17th century as a way of conveying power and grandeur. In 1677, King Louis XIV of France decided to expand a château, or hunting lodge, near Paris and make it the center of his vast kingdom. French architects Louis le Vau (1612–70) and Jules Hardouin Mansart (1646–1708) designed the Palace of Versailles (1661–90) to be overwhelmingly monumental, a symbol of the king's power. The Classical lines of the building are perfectly **symmetrical** and seem to go on forever. This effect is heightened by a large, still pool that reflects the building. The gardens, designed by André Le Nôtre (1613–1700), also appear infinite, arranged in a network of paths that meet at pavilions, fountains, and courtyards. The flowerbeds, trees, and geometrically shaped hedges are organized and symmetrical, complementing the rigid architecture of the palace. Inside, the elaborate decorations and rich materials are as overwhelm-

Diego Velázquez's *Las Meninas* has been considered by many to be the world's greatest painting. Besides studying its artistic and stylistic elements, scholars have also analyzed it from mathematical and political viewpoints.

One of Bernini's architectural masterpieces, the piazza of St. Peter's Basilica was designed to encompass a large area that could hold the crowds that gather here for papal benedictions on Easter and other special occasions.

ing as the scale of the building's exterior. The power of the king is reflected in every aspect of the carefully designed palace.

No one knew the powerful symbolism of architecture better than the Catholic Church. Bernini's grand piazza for St. Peter's Basilica (1657–67) is a symbol of the enduring strength and power of the Church. Two semicircular **colonnades**, each made up of four rows of columns and topped with a row of portrait statues of the saints—96 in all—surround the oval-shaped piazza, which is large enough to hold 300,000 people. The colonnades reach out from the basilica as if to embrace the city beyond. An ancient Egyptian obelisk—a four-sided pillar that tapers at the top—stands in the center of the piazza and points to the heavens, a reminder of God's presence. Bernini intended the piazza to be a fitting introduction to the grandeur of St. Peter's Basilica and a symbol of the Church's influence, extending out into the world.

THE END OF THE BAROQUE PERIOD

Toward the end of the 17th century, the role of art began to change. Instead of being used to teach people or to influence their thoughts, art was primarily something to be admired and enjoyed. Beauty and feeling became the dominant artistic goals. There was a shift away from the rigid Classical style of Poussin and the vigorous realism of Caravaggio toward a warmer, softer style. The new style was called "Rococo," after

Characteristic of the developing Rococo style, Jean Antoine Watteau's *An Embarrassing Proposal* (1719) features beautifully dressed young people idly relaxing against the background of a romantic, pastoral landscape.

THE THIRTY YEARS' WAR

In 1618, the Catholic king Ferdinand II of Bohemia (modern-day Czech and Slovak Republics) began a struggle for religious dominance with the Protestant nobles of his kingdom. Although Ferdinand succeeded in establishing a Catholic Bohemia, the conflict threw off the uneasy balance of power that had been established between Catholics and Protestants in Europe after the Reformation. War enveloped Denmark, Sweden, France, the Netherlands, and Spain over the next 30 years. In 1648, the "Peace of Westphalia" treaties broke up the German empire, established the Netherlands as a republic independent of Spanish rule, and greatly expanded French power.

a type of decorative stonework inspired by shells and other objects from nature. Rococo style carried certain Baroque themes—such as conveying emotion, creating illusions, and theatricality—to new heights of exaggeration. Rococo artists rejected other Baroque characteristics, such as unified compositions, realism, and emphasis on the play of light and shadow.

Painters such as Jean Antoine Watteau (1684–1721) and Jean-Honoré Fragonard (1732–1806), both of France, depicted picturesque landscapes in which delicate, fashionably dressed figures strolled and reclined. Architecture became increasingly extravagant, with dramatic use of light and space. There was a new emphasis on interior decoration; walls, floors, and furniture were covered with rich ornamentation formed by curving, asymmetrical shapes. Birds, flowers, and other natural themes were depicted using rich materials such as stucco, lacquer, and gilt; nature was transformed into a dazzling fantasy world, the perfect setting for the lavish parties and entertainments of the period.

These changes were caused in part by a new distinction between public and private art. Instead of being confined to churches, palaces, and other public spaces, art found a new market in private homes. This innovation had already arrived in Holland, where a large, wealthy middle class created great demand for domestic scenes and paintings of fruit and flowers. In France, it took a different turn. Instead of catering to middle-class taste, private art in France was an expression of elegance. Wealthy art collectors and home owners wanted to show off their fashionable taste.

The decadence of Rococo was also fueled by the desire for luxurious comfort. The period was notable for the unashamed display of wealth and the freedom to wallow in it. The triumph of centralized monarchy had

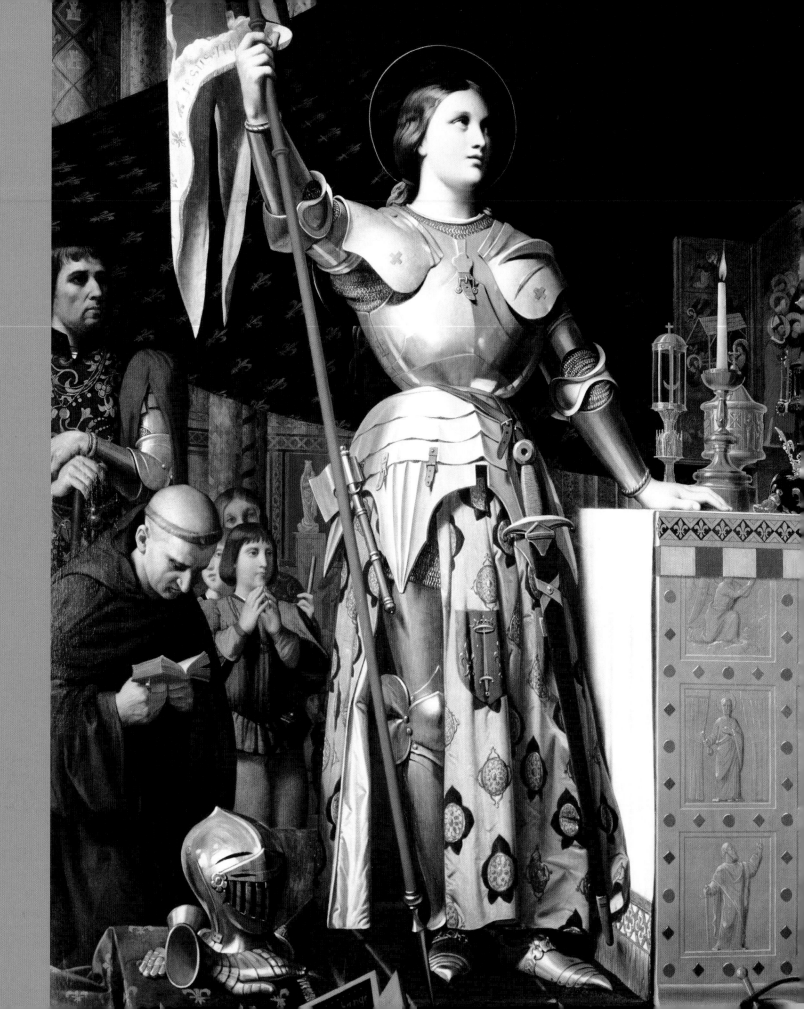

given rise to the idea that kings ruled by "divine right"—they were chosen to rule by God. For some, this idea also gave them the right to do as they wished with their power. The son of Louis XIV, Louis XV, and his mistress, Madame de Pompadour, were lavish patrons of the arts. But Louis XV was a particularly weak ruler who paid more attention to his life of pleasure than affairs of state. Matters grew worse during the reign of Louis XVI, whose wife, Marie-Antoinette, built an Arcadian village, complete with a lake and a flock of perfumed sheep, at the Palace of Versailles, where she spent vast sums of money on elaborate parties.

In 1789, the excesses of the French monarchy led to a bloody revolution. The king and many other nobles were beheaded, and a republic was established. In the years that followed, Rococo style and its close cousin, Baroque, were associated with the excesses of the aristocracy and fell into disfavor. As they had at the beginning of the 17th century, artists sought reform and found the answer in Classicism. The Neo-Classical movement embodied reason, secularism, and revolutionary political ideals. It was not until the end of the 19th century that Neo-Classical disdain gave way to a new appreciation for Baroque art.

Many of the great Baroque artists became important influences for their later countrymen. Poussin influenced French painters Jean-Auguste Ingres (1780–1867) and Paul Cézanne (1839–1906). Rembrandt is regarded as the central figure of a "Golden Age" in Dutch painting. Spanish painter Francisco Goya (1746–1828) named Velázquez as one of his influences, and another Spaniard, Pablo Picasso (1881–1973), said, "Velázquez, when all is said and done, he's the best." Baroque was an international style, but each region's

The inspiration of Baroque artists can be seen in many works by Jean-Auguste Ingres (above). His *Joan of Arc at the Coronation of Charles VII in Reims Cathedral* (1854, opposite) depicts the 17-year-old warrior dressed in armor as she witnesses the king's coronation ceremony. Interestingly, Ingres chose not to picture King Charles in the painting.

artists took Baroque style in a different direction. It was subdued and intellectual in France, intimate and domestic in the Netherlands, and courtly and richly colored in Spain. The term "Baroque" encompasses a great variety. In some ways, the differences that emerged during this period marked the beginning of distinctive national styles.

The Baroque period also saw the founding of the Academy of Painting and Sculpture (later named the École des Beaux-arts) in 1648 in Paris and 1666

Vue perspective du Sallon de l'Academie Royale de Peinture et de Sculpture au Louvre à Paris.

in Rome. The Academy emphasized studying Classical art and copying great masterpieces of the past as the foundation of an artist's education. During the 17th century, it was the forum in which great debates were held over which was more important: line or color. Those who argued for line were called Poussinistes, while the color-enthusiasts were known as Rubenistes. For the next 200 years, the Academy was the leader of artistic trends and the judge and guardian of artistic taste. In the 19th century, Academy painting was the establishment against which Impressionist painters rebelled, holding the "Salon des Refusés" to exhibit paintings that were refused by the Academy.

The artistic debates of the Baroque period laid the foundation for many of the issues that every generation of artists must confront anew, such as the relative importance of line and color, whether depiction should be realistic or expressive, and the choice between the harmony of a unified composition or the dramatic effect of breaking the rules. Different sides have won at different times in the eternal arguments. The unique contribution of the Baroque period to these discussions has left an enduring legacy of great art that will continue to fascinate, provoke, and entertain for generations to come.

Influencing not only traditional art forms such as painting and sculpture, the Baroque period also had an impact on furniture designs. But as Rococo art began to spread, so, too, did a new style of furniture (above), marked by a lighter and more graceful style than Baroque furniture.

TIMELINE

1597	Caravaggio begins painting scenes from the life of St. Matthew for the Contarelli Chapel
1598	Caracci begins work on the ceiling frescoes of Palazzo Farnese in Rome
1600	The first opera, *Euridice*, is written and performed in Florence, Italy
1601	Caravaggio paints *Supper at Emmaus*
1606	Caravaggio kills a man and flees Rome
1614	Rubens completes the *Descent from the Cross*
1618	The Thirty Years' War begins
1619	The first slaves arrive in North America
1623	Velázquez becomes court painter to Philip IV of Spain
1629	Poussin's altarpiece for St. Peter's Cathedral is received with disfavor
	Bernini becomes the official architect for St. Peter's Basilica
1630	Rubens paints *Peace and War* for King Charles I of England
1633	Galileo is charged with heresy and placed under house arrest
1635	Rembrandt paints *Belshazzar's Feast*
1638	Poussin paints *The Arcadian Shepherds*
1643	Louis XIV becomes king of France
1648	The Thirty Years' War ends with the Peace of Westphalia
	The Academy of Painting and Sculpture is founded in Paris
1652	Bernini completes the *Ecstasy of St. Theresa*
1656	Velázquez paints *Las Meninas*
1661	Work begins on the Palace of Versailles
1667	The piazza of St. Peter's Basilica is completed
1682	Louis XIV moves his court to Versailles
1687	English scientist Sir Isaac Newton publishes his theories on physics, gravity, and the universe
1715	Louis XIV dies, and Louis XV becomes king of France

GLOSSARY

altarpieces	ornamental paintings or carvings placed above and behind an altar
anatomy	the structure of a living thing, especially the human body
apprenticed	made an assistant to an artist, working in exchange for instruction in artistic technique
chapel	a room or recess in a church with its own altar, used for special services
Classical	relating to Roman and Greek culture from about 500 B.C. to about A.D. 500
colonize	to establish a settlement in a distant land, subject to the political control of the settlers' native land
colonnades	a series of columns placed at regular intervals in a straight or curving line, supporting a roof
commission	request for a work of art to be made to order, in exchange for money
compositions	arrangements of the parts of a work of art to create a unified, harmonious appearance for each piece
decadent	excessively self-indulgent
diplomat	a representative of a government who conducts relations with the governments of other nations
fresco	painting made on wet plaster with watercolors, so that when the plaster dries the paint crystallizes on the wall
gilt	a thin covering of gold
nobles	people who hold inherited wealth, political power, and social position; also known as aristocrats or the aristocracy
patron	a wealthy person who supports an artist financially and gives him or her commissions
perspective	the changed appearance of objects according to their distance and position
realism	realistic depiction
republic	a state or nation governed by representatives who are elected by the citizens
self-portraits	paintings or drawings in which the artist depicts himself or herself
symmetrical	shaped or arranged similarly on both sides of an imaginary line

INDEX